AF484985

Stillness
in the Psalms

ISBN: 9798995625612
Published by: Alegria Publishing
Book cover and layout by: @mckadamia

Stillness in the Psalms

ANASTASIA LINDSEY

ALEGRÍA
PUBLISHING

The Way Through the Water

Lord,

Lift me up as I write.
Guard me from distraction and discouragement.
Cover my mind with clarity,
my heart with peace,
and my spirit with fire for You.
Let every word I write
be anointed with Your presence,
so that my readers don't just see poetry—
they encounter You.
Keep me rested, replenished, and renewed.
Break every chain of exhaustion and fear,
and replace it with joy, light, and holy confidence.
Let this book be a lighthouse,
drawing the lost safely to shore.

Amen

Welcome to Saltwater Psalms!

Within these many pages, you will find poems, prayers, and surrender. I fell victim to believing that my prayers had to be perfect but I realize that is far from the truth. They just have to be real. Saltwater Psalms takes the prayers I have said, the poems I have written, and the tears I have cried into the palms of God's hands and dives deep into the real conversations that many of us suppress.

I hope you find His light in between these lines to help you get through your toughest moments. Some poems and prayers are full of tears and others are soaked in peace - highlighting the duality of human nature. I hope these feel like a soothing balm for the soul and a softness to calm your anxious heart.

May this book meet you right where you are and lead you gently into the arms of God.

With so much love,

Anastasia

Hi—my name is Anastasia,
a name that means resurrection,
or she who shall rise again.
like the sun,
I rise each morning—
ready to embody the miracle
of being alive.
my poetry holds the echoes
of every time I too rose
after being pushed down
too far.
and now,
it's my life's mission
to teach others how to rise.
I'm soft-spoken,
but some people make me come alive—
pulling me from behind my poetic lines.
my heart beats like thunder,
but truly,
I thrive when the rain covers me gently.

I'm sensitive—
enough for both of us, actually.

that also means
I'll shield your heart
with mine.
I'll stretch my arms wide,
as far east as they'll reach,
to keep you safe from pain.

you can find me
basking in birdsong
outside my bedroom window,
learning new recipes,
and tucked beneath warm blankets
devouring the latest romance release.

I'm a hopeful romantic,
infatuated with love—
its quiet corners and epic chapters.
I'll ask you if you're happy,
then gently nudge you to share
the story of your greatest
love adventure.

yes, I cry easily.
yes, I ask the rain
to go easy on me.
but I'll love you
like you've never been loved before.

I ask too many questions—
only because I care.

I am full of fire,
though you might not see it.
I'm surrounded by water,
born on a rainy spring day.
I am
passionate, driven—
maybe a little too much.
but I ride the waves
like I've been surfing for lifetimes.

I am an adventurer,
a traveler,
a seeker—
yet I find peace
knowing my garden is waiting
at home.

I love cozy corners, warmth,
and the shape of small things.
I will hold your fingertips in my palms
until they are warm again.

there's more to me
than meets the eye—
but I'm the girl who memorizes
the color of your eyes,
just to tell you
how beautiful they are.

//

There was a moment that changed it all:

a collection of tiny moments
led me here.
to believe,
to the arms of God,
to this unshakable faith I now carry
like breath.

it started in my grandmother's hands,
the way she clutched her rosary—
glossy beads clicking like whispered promises,
the silver cross pressed with reverence,
a capsule of holy water
tucked in like a secret.
now I hold it too.
and when I do—
I smell her perfume,
I feel her presence.
I hear the echo of the prayers
she once whispered over me
while I slept.

it was the first time
I watched The Passion Of Christ,
my pillow soaked in tears,
my face wet with the weight
of a love that bled for me.
I cried so hard,
the salt stung my skin.
but I wept for the One

who wept for me first.

it was the sound of someone saying,
don't give up
on the exact day
I wanted to.
On the days I whispered, God I can't keep going
He sent someone to say, *because of you I still am*

it wasn't one single moment -
it was all of them.
the scent of my grandmother's room,
the sound of rosary beads in her lap,
the taste of tears,
the feel of hands on mine,
the soft nudge of compassion
when I could've collapsed.

these small moments—
stitched belief into me.
not loudly.
but deeply.
and now, here I stand—
not because I found God all at once,
but because He found me
in a thousand tiny ways.

//

prayer

poor me -
speaking to the Lord again
His hands so heavily placed
on the edge of my shoulders.
the weight of guilt once heavy
feels light to His presence.
today is possible -
tomorrow has blown away
yet it still remains tangled in my thoughts
like holiday lights
piled in dust covered boxes
He is light,
a collection of safe spaces
and the reason why water
holds the corners of the Earth.
and fear consumes me why?
so I pray to the Lord again
my collection of clustered fears
bundled tight like picked daisies.
what does He do?
plucks the petals one by one
"does she trust me?"
"does she trust me not?"
I wish to be the petal
that trusts,
so that my seeds can bear
beautiful fruit.

//

I know He is present today -

the birds outside my window
chirp a little louder
the sun I feel on my skin
is just a little bit warmer.
the food I eat,
that more fulfilling.
poems I write come to life
they grow feet and walk His path -
taking my hand and
leading the way.
people in passing smile more,
they share a glance
that only tells me one thing -
they see Jesus inside of me
as I do in them.

//

Welcome to your first Holy Water Page

This is where you pause. This is where your tears become prayers. A page for cleansing thoughts and sacred time with God. You don't have to have the words so there will be some provided below for you. You only have to bring yourself. Let this page hold what you can no longer carry. The Lord is with you!

✝ God, please heal my heart. My soul is tired and my heart is growing weak. I believe that You can heal me!

✝ God, surprise me with joy in moments where I least expect it!

✝ God, when my world grows loud, help me to find rest in Your quiet presence. Help me to lean on You when my thoughts overwhelm me!

✝ God, help me slow down. I have been moving too fast and I'm afraid my life is slipping by. Help me to see that my life is a gift worth cherishing!

✝ God, prepare my heart for the goodness You have in store for me. I trust that You are the author of my story and plan things for my highest well-being!

✝ God, when it feels like too much, and I can't keep going, be the footsteps in the sand, carrying my weary soul and healing my aching heart. Please steady my soul so that I may find peace!

✝ God, remind me that I am Your child and that You will never abandon me. I believe You hold me in the palm of Your hands!

✝ God, please take away my pain, heal the hurt that I carry, and bring light to the darkness that surrounds me. I am a child of the light and am protected by Your mercy!

Please feel free to say your own or quietly reflect with God!

    prayer can be
closed eyes
and a silent mouth.
it can be run-on sentences
and punctuation free.
prayer can be
song,
spoken word,
or even hands holding onto hope.
it can be eyes that look
past the clouds,
and hands that reach for the sun.
prayer can be
worship on Sunday
and tears in the shower on Saturday.
it can be a walk with no destination,
or noticing the moon again.
prayer can be a sigh,
for He knows what's on the heart
it can be a drawing,
or words tangled on string.
prayer can be
the art of just being.

//

    may the reader
holding this book
reading this poem,
be planted like the wildflowers
along the roadside.
may this reader be planted
by Your grace
and watered by your goodness.
I ask that you help them grow,
in their body, their home,
feeling safe in your presence.
may their beauty never be hidden,
and I ask that their soul,
be a reminder of hope
for others to keep going.
pull them through any dirt
they may find themselves in
and bring them to the light.
may they continue to bloom
basking in the sunlight,
and unfold with each day
to new and miraculous wonders.
I ask that the day greet them
as morning dew covers the grass
and the sun reaches through
the trees.
Amen

//

I want to live -
I don't watch the sunrise,
and more times than not
I eat in a rush -
letting the steam
burn the roof of my mouth.
I forget to pray,
and lounge instead of going for a walk.
my plants haven't been watered
in a few days,
I, too, am a little dehydrated.
I stopped singing in the shower
and have purposely avoided
taking pictures.
I wonder if my desire to travel
overseas will stop being but a dream.
I'm afraid to cry
that's a lie, I cry
but I hide my face from others.

I want to forgive,
but I hold onto pain longer than I should.
somehow I have convinced myself
that cupcakes are bad
and brownies add on the pounds
but in the middle of that,
I stopped celebrating the good
        stopped celebrating myself.
I want to live,
God, please show me
how to slow down,
to savor this life
You have so freely given me.
to do the things,
be bold and daring,
watch the sunset,
pray...
and eat the dang cupcake.

//

God seems to know
the ache of my soul
that hasn't yet found words.
He seems to already be aware
of my pain
before pain itself even knows.
how does He do that?

//

       prayer changes things
it's a shock to the heart
that gets it beating again.
prayer gets the blood going
a warmup before a workout.
prayer is a vacation away
from living with a broken spirit.
it reminds you of your breath
like a breeze in the hot summer sun.
prayer is like the first bite
of creme brule
it covers the buds
and soothes the soul.
in fact, prayer surrounds you
and covers your entirety.
prayer is peace,
in the middle of a war.

//

they say change is the only constant,
I say God is.
change is inevitable,
but God is possible!

//

sometimes I think about living a long life
but really, I just want a full life.
I want my days to be filled with laughter
and the smiles of my nieces and nephews.
I want to indulge in lightly salted popcorn
at midnight with my husband.
I want puppy dog tails
to bruise my legs
when I arrive home from a long day at work.
I want peace and happiness to spill
out of me
all over me
and back into me again.
I want to hear my mother's voice
and hug my siblings' necks.
I want to write poetry
on a balcony in Italy,
and see my husband's brown eyes
in the heat of the roma sun.
a long life, full of I love you's
to family and friends
and food that heals the soul.

//

Normalize asking people what God has been up to in their lives. I challenge you to ask one person this!

//

God gathers for me wildflowers
a compilation of all my favorites.
He knows the days when my soul
longs for scents of lilies and lavender
and when my eyes need pops of yellow.
He says I too am like a wildflower
blooming in my own time,
dancing in the sunlight.
He too says I was made to bring beauty
to this place,
to be delicate and strong.

//

God,
with Your strength, I can climb
with Your love, I am protected
with Your peace, I am free
with Your mercy, I am forgiven
with Your grace, I am loved.
with my eyes on You, I am never lost.

//

    growing up,
I thought God only resided in church.
that if I spoke to Him -
He wouldn't hear me
unless my spoken words were
whispered in a church pew.
as an adult I realize,
that He is the God
of an unmade bed,
always there in the mess,
there in the rush,
there in the to-do lists.
He's there when my alarm goes off,
there when I snooze,
there when I pull the covers
back over my head.
God can hear me in my sleep
as much as he can in a church pew.

//

even a whispered amen
finds its way to the ears of God -
never doubt the power
of quiet faith.
surely, even your softest prayers
echo in heaven.

//

Instructions on how & when to talk to God -

in the middle of a breakdown
while giving birth
at the first sip of coffee
when your eyes first open
in silence
at a concert
before going to sleep
while holding back tears
when you find yourself angry
at the first bite of cake
in the office
when you have no words to say
when you have too much to say
when you can
however you can
because He is always listening
even here,
even now.

//

     pain in the body,
tremble in the hands,
shaking at the knee's -
wanting to be so close
to Jesus -
to only touch but a piece
of His garment.
not his hand, nor his skin,
          -    His garment.
the edges worn from
dust and time,
the cloth rugged
with no smooth edges.
not a shout of His name,
but a reach with my hand,
to touch but a piece
of His garment.
from the rawest part
of my faith,
from the deepest part
of me inside,
that believe miracles do exist,
I touched His garment -
and healing came from
He who saw not my shame,
not my suffering,
just my faith.

//

I believed that my tears
were a sign of weakness,
until I read that Jesus wept.
the sky did not flinch,
the Earth did not scold him,
the world did not end -
He wept.
what a holy thing,
to carry such emotion -
such care and divine sensitivity
for people and entire cities.
Jesus, deeply human, deeply feeling
who they still called Messiah
wept!

when my own tears come,
I do not shame them,
because Jesus wept too.
Jesus is my river,
I shall be like the stream.
both sensitive, both sacred
letting tears soothe the rugged stones.
my tears are holy -
never heavy.

//

A prayer for the sensitive ones:

Thank You, God, for this soft, swelling heart. Thank You for showing me that weeping is not weakness, it's worship and it's feeling. Let my tenderness be a testimony that You are alive within me. Let my emotions be part of Your ministry. Let my tears water the land and show the world Your holiness.

Amen

Stillness in the Psalms

when the miracle feels out of sight
when it seems like God
has gone quiet toward my heart -
as if my dreams I've desired
may never come true -
I redirect my thoughts.
not only is He preparing *me* for it,
He's preparing *it* for me too.
I can't imagine the work it takes
to shape a soul like mine.
so full of doubt,
tangled with mistrust
heavy with fear,
and at times a lack of faith.

I can't imagine the work it takes
to prepare dreams as grand as mine -
they stretch past the oceans,
are taller than mountains,
they are mighty!
I then remember,
He is too.
and if my dreams
align with his will
then they are not only possible,
they are promised.

//

I trust in His promise,
not His pace.
His timeline,
not mine.
may I never grow bitter in the waiting,
but bolder in the possible.

Jesus,
meet me in the gap -
the space in between my belief
and unbelief.
between my hope in Your timing
and my hesitation.

//

we are lilies in the light,
rooted in God's soil.
only blooming
by His grace that lifts us upward.
because of Him,
we can.
the light draws us up
in our darkest moments.
how beautiful it is
to unfold our petals
before His gaze.
to stretch our petals before Him,
our Saviour.
in a field full of lilies,
He sees each one of us -
never forgotten in the field,
nor overlooked by shadows.
we are lilies
held by the light
and named by love.

//

we are more than our mistakes
more than our sorrow -
for under the sun
we are alive and growing.
we are being nurtured
beyond what our eyes can see.
our hearts in sync
with the rays of the sun.
this life is fleeting -
a vapor, a whisper
that holds a magnitude of beauty.
we are light-drenched souls
wandering through this time
under the sun.
what we do with this time
it matters.
who we are under this sun
it matters.

this journey is a sacred walk -
when we pause to feel
the sacredness in every bloom,
we quiet our mind to grace.
there is a love
that lives beyond the sun
and we can tap into it
        not someday
but now!
yes, under this beautiful sun
we are held by something greater
than our weaknesses,
something greater than our faults.
all because of
the goodness of God.

//

Holy Water Page

Take your time with each one. You do not have to journal them all at once!

Journaling prompts:

- What is your relationship with God like?
- When it comes to God, I am still learning how to....
- Write a prayer for someone who will never know you prayed for them
- What are you holding onto that needs to be laid down?
- How can you pray for yourself today?
- Have you felt the presence of God lately?
- Do you believe in miracles? What miracle are you in need of?
- Is there something you would like to forgive yourself for?

Stillness

in the Psalms

they called me names
that didn't belong to me.
I answered still -
afraid of what my silence might do.
I have been mistaken,
overlooked,
judged.
a tornado, creating mess
with everything my hands ever touched.
they tore me down with their words
what they thought about me,
I believed,
carried pain that was never
mine to claim.
but God....
when I fell into troubled waters
He did not let me go.
He cupped the waves into His hands
and washed my fear away.
but God....

He healed my heart,
wiped clean their words,
that I was never meant to believe.
their opinions may echo,
but God's voice takes over.
He says,
I love you
& you are mine.
there is no one else,
He'd rather I be.
God never misnamed me,
yet counted every strand of hair
on my head.
He claimed my blueprint
before the world
tried to redraw it.
He knit me -
intricately created,
wonderfully made.
He did the same for you!

//

love is patient,
love is kind
 - not only when you're shining
but also,
when you're falling apart too.
even when your worth
slips through the cracks
of your weak and trembling hands,
or when you fumble in the dark,
this love stays.

//

He sees -
although He may feel far,
He is near.
every worry captured
in the creases of your palms
He sees.
there is not a part
of your body,
that Jesus will ever reject.
He meets us where we are,
shattered and scared -
He says fear not,
for I am at your side.
hitting rock bottom
only pushes us closer
into the arms of Christ.
that is where healing takes place -

//

Holywater page

"Come to me, all who are weary and burdened, and I will give you rest."
-Matthew 11:28

Let's use this opportunity to reflect on, by far, one of my favorite parts in Scripture. As someone who has frequently felt weary and burdened, this always gave me peace.

1. Where are you carrying weight, you were never meant to hold?
2. What if I told you, rest is freely yours, not something earned?
3. What if I told you that Jesus accepts all of you? Even your exhaustion. How would you respond?
4. Are you willing to give Jesus your exhaustion today and allow Him to renew your strength?

It's okay to give Him your exhaustion, your mess, your storms, your inner critic, your aches & pain. He wants it all. Allow Him to show up in your life as you surrender to the rest that is so freely given to us. His arms are the best place to be. Close your eyes and imagine Jesus holding you close. Lay yourself down, so He can lift you up.

Stillness in the Psalms

    what is meant for me
will never slip through the cracks
of these hands
because they are in the palms of Jesus.
dipped in His glory,
blessed with His mercy,
and stamped with His love.
my eyes are on Jesus,
the one who breathes my dreams
into existence.
I cling onto Him only,
not my own agenda,
nor my own timelines,
only Him who clings onto my dreams.
what is meant for me
is sealed in His glory.
what's mine is carefully held
by the one who is holding me.

//

In Proverbs 4:23
we are told to *guard our hearts*
for everything you do flows from it
guard your heart -
not because it's weak,
but because He created it.
every part of it,
flows from his everlasting love.
your heart,
like a well -
may it never run dry.
make your heart a resting place
for those who thirst for the love
of Jesus.

//

oh, when I see Jesus,
when I meet Him face to face,
I will eagerly embrace His arms,
I will cry tears
more than I had my whole life.
I will watch as my heartbeat
extends out of my chest,
I will pour myself onto Him,
a moment I waited forever for.
Jesus, He who gave me
the greatest life
and blessed me beyond measure,
cannot wait to spend eternity with me.
what a lucky girl I am!

//

one day,
you will look back -
& see He carried you though it all.
the moments when the light
seemed far away,
His light was guiding your heart.
the moments when waters
seemed too deep,
He was your lighthouse.
the moments when fear
seemed too big for defeat,
He was the protector of your soul.
His name alone, protects -
His name alone, heals -
His name alone, soothes -
His name alone, calms.
His name alone, is love.

//

start again,
are the words He said to me.
when my hands were bruised
my heart was broken,
and ash covered my soul.
start again,
are the words He said to me.
when they left me behind,
called me names that stung,
and weapons were formed against me.

He knew the plans,
the opportunities,
because He planned them.
start again,
it wasn't just a declaration,
but a promise that He would deliver me.

//

Holy Water Page

Let's take a moment to pause and be with the Lord. Light a candle and sit with Him— not to perform, not to strive, but simply to be. Whether your heart is overflowing with words or completely empty, this space is for you. You don't need perfect prayers or polished thoughts, just your presence. If you're too tired to speak, He still hears you. If all you have is silence or pain, He feels it fully. Let this be a moment where you let go of holding it all together. Close your eyes. Breathe. Let Him hold you. Let this time be soft and healing. And when you're ready — whether you write, rest, or read on — may your heart feel lighter, your mind more at peace, and your spirit reminded that you are deeply seen, heard, and loved. You are in my prayers.

If your heart is silent, here are a few prompts you are welcome to use as you speak to Him.

→ What is this moment in my life teaching me?
→ How can I serve You, Lord, for myself and for others?
→ What are You forming in me during this season of silence?
→ Am I leaning into my own understanding, or resting in Yours?
→ What am I holding onto that You want me to release into Your hands?
→ Lord, how are you revealing Yourself in this moment of silence?

Stillness in the Psalms

     believing in God
doesn't mean the storms won't come.
believing in God
means when the storms do come
we have everything we need.
there will be
no emergency runs to the store,
panic buying bread
to cure our hunger.
or aimlessly searching for batteries,
to bring back the light,
He provides it all.
He not only calms the storms,
but walks with us through them.

//

my steps are planned,
drawing me near His purpose
for my life.
my maps, I no longer need,
the checklists, irrelevant.
I want what He wants for me-
for He knows the plans He has for me.
when I stopped trusting my plan,
and began trusting His word,
that's when my life changed.

//

where does my faith come from, you ask?
it was always there,
but my awareness of it was not.
my faith was birthed,
breathed into me
in silence,
in sorrow,
in searching.
it came in flickers,
in the smile of a stranger,
in the ache that made me reach upward,
in the stillness after the storm.
yes, my family planted seeds,
but it was I
who had to water them
with my own tears.
I had to search high and wide,
dig deep into days that felt hollow,
and still believe
He was near,
even when He felt far,
when my faith felt like fog
and my prayers an echo.

but He was writing inside of me all along,
He, an author so holy
placed faith into my story
before I knew how to name it.
it was in the plot twists,
the heartbreaks,
the miracles,
the waiting rooms.

He wrote faith into my lifeline,
into my lungs.
and when I fell to my knees,
 it wasn't a breaking,
 it was finding what I had inside all along.

now I spend my days
chasing the One
who was never far from me.
basking in what
was already within me
all along.

//

I want to feel close to God, where do I start?

- Whisper, God, I want to know You
- Open your eyes in the morning with a heart full of gratitude
- Close them at night with love in your heart
- Ask for forgiveness
- Pray!
- Listen to worship music
- Read His word
- Offer kindness to others
- Forgive others
- Be messy, be human, be real (He knows you!)
- Go for a walk

You can find God wherever you are. Open your eyes and ears to the wonders all around you. I promise, finding Him isn't what we think it's like. Turn around, He's already there - you just have to let him in.

//

Prayer:

let every false name fall away.
let every wound find Your word.
let me walk in the truth
that I am Yours—
and that is always enough.
may Your words override theirs,
and may my ears only yearn
to hear Your truth.
Amen

//

        for 365 days,
I clenched tightly to a steering wheel
knuckles white, and a tear stained face.
I prayed for better,
for saving,
for new.
my home was not a refuge,
work was not a sanctuary,
and each time I left either,
it was leaving one storm,
and walking into another.
my temple - hollow,
my mind - blank,
my heart - broken into pieces.
I rolled out of bed each morning,
only allowing myself just enough time
to dress my wounds with routine.
only a few seconds to appear presentable,
but my interior was bruised and battered.
in that 25-minute commute,
knuckles white, a tear stained face,
I carried a mustard seed -
small enough to slip through these fingers
at any given moment.
yet, mighty it was,
to anchor me in His truth.

it would have been easy to say,
365 days, the Lord does not hear me.
it would have been easy to accept
that His silence meant His absence.
the Holy Spirit whispered,
He is here.
I kept going,
kept believing,
holding on.
not by my own strength,
but because He was there!
His gentle presence
was but a slight breath of air
that soothed my exhaustion.
when the promise came,
I realized that every tear,
He saw.
every 25-minute commute,
He was there.
every ache,
He held tightly.
the road to and from,
was only the pavement of His love.
His silence was only a seed -
that needed time to grow

//

I was never meant to fit in -
in a world that has lost its
taste for Jesus
I was made to bring back the flavor of Him.
I carry salt in my soul,
allowing Him to use me as ocean spray.
scattering His word in forgotten places
and bland parts of land.
salt heals wounds -
makes us thirsty,
the type of quench that can only
be fulfilled by the psalms.
I pray He keeps me different
and always thirsty for His living water.
the salt of the Earth,
sprinkling love onto every person I meet,
showing them the flavor of His heart.

//

His love, planted deep within -
wrapped and climbed my ribs
like vines that bloom in sunlight.
He planted a seed in my heart,
called it by the name love,
and watched it grow wild.
now there is a garden
blooming in my soul.

but like my sensitive nature,
I got watered too -
mouthfuls of rain water,
my heart heavy with tears.
not to endure pain,
but to cure the drought
of another's aching soul.
storms and wind,
or sweet morning dew,
it's still Him, working through
me, to be better for you.

He is the living Word -
an endless supply I draw from,
dipping my pen
in Heaven's inkwell
to write this book for us.

//

Jesus is the sunrise
that spills across my broken pieces.
the light of the world -
the rays of the sun.
He is the painter of dusk and dawn,
a cathedral of stained glass.
every crack of my soul,
each fracture of my frail body,
His horizon covers me.
my scars glow
soft beneath His touch.
what has broken me,
then became His canvas -
for no amount of darkness
can keep me hidden from His sight.
as He splits the sky open,
I'm reminded why mornings
whisper His glory.

//

life, at times, can be bitter -
sour notes linger just a little longer,
the lemons dealt - spoiled.
but there is a richness found in God,
a certain sweetness that takes
spoiled lemons and makes them whole again.
sometimes, the joys of life
are like sugar in lemonade -
here one moment, then quickly dissolves.
but there is a soothing element in God,
a certain mercy that coats us in love,
like honey covering the soul.
when I speak His words,
I taste peace, I savor His Truth.
the spoiled lemons in my life,
the sour taste of pain,
the bitter moments,
are all soothed by Him -
the one who nourishes me
back to health.

//

In John 6:35, Jesus said,
I am the bread of life;
Whoever comes to me shall not hunger,
And whoever believes in me
Shall never thirst.

there is plenty of bread to go around,
for you, for me, for every family.
when all you see are crumbs,
He comes bearing more.
there is no starvation worse
than not being filled by Jesus.
every bite of His presence,
is a taste for life itself.
broken things,
broken bread,
are filled with nothing but Him.

//

Holy Water Page:

Music has always been a way that I relate to myself, the world, and even with my faith. There are so many songs that I could add to this page for you to listen to but I know He will lead you to the songs that will be marked as a favorite on your very own playlists.

For the time being, I wanted to share some of the softest songs that healed me. From the lyrics to the tunes, I could feel the presence of Him.

You can listen to these songs however you wish, whether it is a walk in the park, while doing chores, on your daily commute, or before falling asleep. Feel free to write about the ones that touched you and the experiences you had with them. These experiences are good to look back on when you're having a day where hope seems absent.

Point your camera to the code to bring up the playlist & enjoy! You can come back to this playlist as many times as you would like. I will continue to add songs along the way!

Scan me!

Here are some prompts that you can journal while you listen!

✝ Are there any songs that speak to your heart?

✝ Which song had a lyric that felt specific to you?

✝ What is a rhythm or lyric that seems to echo your current season of life?

✝ How can you bring more stillness, gratitude, or worship into your week?

✝ As the melody unfolds, what memory surfaces? Why do you think God brought that to mind right now?

we are but clay -
sculpted, crafted, perfected
all by His fingerprints.
every ridge of His finger,
every spiral, loop and swirl,
etched into all living beings.
we were touched by the Maker's hand -
what a beautiful blessing to have.
His identity - pressed
into every fragile corner
of the human soul.
may we see each other
as walking prints of God.

//

to walk amongst a garden -
is to walk amongst the breath of God.
every petal, a whisper of grace,
every stem, a promise rooted in hope.
as the lilies move with the wind,
and the roses unwind with the breeze,
we realize -
it is not just the wind,
but the breath of God is near.
He is just as close,
as the air we breathe -
He IS the air we breathe,
the fragrance of the flowers we admire.

//

each morning,
I looked in the mirror
and watched myself fade.
not in body,
but in soul.
a little less light each day,
a little more shadow.
a little less love,
a little more hate.
I was shrinking
under the weight of cruelty
in a place that did not welcome me.
sadness wore me down.
frustration frayed my edges
I began to believe
the lie that I was less,
that I was unseen,
that being God's beloved
wasn't enough to keep me safe from their words.

I trusted how they viewed me,
over the real truth,
that God loves me.
I stopped taking care of myself,
allowed God's light within to dim,
day by day.

and when the day finally came
to walk away,
I carried hurt like a weapon,
my hands shaking over a keyboard,
ready to strike back
with a letter sharp enough
to wound them as I had been wounded.

but then—
His voice.
soft. steady. sovereign.
close the laptop
in that holy pause,
revenge unclenched its fists.
in that silence,
my chains fell to the floor.
I realized vengeance
was never my calling

—healing was.
the darkest moment
wasn't the mirror,
it was what I almost became.
and the transformation?
choosing to let Him
rewrite my ending.
I walked away,
not broken,
but becoming.
not bitter,
but beloved.
not forgotten,
but found.

//

She lost faith in God when...

- The person she believed to love her, left,

- Her baby was sick for days and help never arrived,

- Her dog of 14 years crossed the rainbow bridge,

- Her mother's cancer diagnosis came back,

- The car she just paid off broke down,

- A house she dreamed of raising a family in burned down,

- When she lost her job without notice,

- She had her 3rd miscarriage.

open your heart to God
if you are losing faith in Him.
one thing about the God we have,
is that he will never shame your honest feelings.
Jesus is here to show us the way,
as we are never meant to do this alone,
or even rely on our own strength.

//

His love knew no other way,
so forgiveness He freely gave us.
not because we earned it,
but because His love was greater.
before the first tear could trace your cheek,
you were already forgiven.
before the guilt formed its walls in your heart,
His grace had already gone ahead of you.
this, my friend,
is the way of God.
His forgiveness is not a transaction,
but a gift that flows from the cross.
our tears of repentance are but a stream,
that flows directly to Him.
we are called into His current,
to forgive as we have been forgiven,
like Peter -
not seven times, but seventy.
forgiveness is freedom,
it breaks our rusted chains
of bitterness,
resentment,

and opens locked doors.
it's not always easy,
a task that feels uncomfortable -
scary.
in those times,
look through His eyes.
the very same eyes that saw your sin,
and still called you beloved.
speak through His lips,
the same lips that said
Father, forgive them
to a world that pierced Him.
forgiveness isn't forgetting,
nor excusing,
it's releasing.
it's welcoming Christ into your heart,
and handing those wounds
into the palm of His hands.
into the hands of the Healer
He who repairs what we cannot.

//

there is something I call the *Holy Pause*
a sacred stillness,
when the saying *God knows best*
takes full force.
in every second of our lives,
at our deepest, most fragile moments,
God is at work
behind the scenes.

He knows the next step
before it crosses my mind.
He knows when danger is approaching
before I rise in the morning.
it's in those moments when God
steps in on our behalf
and pauses my mind,
the thoughts that arise from emotions,
and guides me to turn towards Him.

//

Holy Water Page:

Scripture: Psalm 103:12: *"As far as the east from the west, so far has He removed our transgressions from us."*

Look what He has done here! Took our sins and placed them at an infinite distance away from us. Talk about forgiveness. Our sins are not held against us. The boundless grace that is given to us is something to revel in. I can't fathom that at times. When I allow myself to sit with my mistakes and sins, I wonder how I could be forgiven, but I am. What that does to my heart I can't put into words!

When we forgive others, we aren't denying the hurt we felt, but instead, handing over our wounds to the Healer, and entrusting Him to take care of us. Forgiveness gives us freedom, to break from the chains and rebuke any bitterness that may take root in our soul. Step into God's mercy when you go to forgive, the same mercy that rushed to us.

Prayer: Lord, help me forgive as You have forgiven me. When resentment clings to my soul, replace it with Your holy release. When my heart is heavy, flood it with Your peace. When forgiveness won't leave my lips, show me the same eyes that saw me with grace, not because they deserve it but because You have shown me grace beyond measurement. Thank You for the gift of forgiveness. In Jesus name, amen!

Journal

1. Who comes to your mind when you think of forgiveness?

2. What wound are you still carrying that Jesus is asking you to place in His hands?

3. How would your life feel if you let Him carry the weight of any burdens you feel?

Affirmation: As You have forgiven me, Lord, so too may I forgive.

here I stand,
imperfectly human.
flesh and bone,
clay and oxygen.
God's fingerprints -
pressed into the clay of my soul,
etched into the marrow of my bones.
when my edges feel rugged,
my surface far from smooth,
it is not failure,
but the Potter at work.
He forms me, shapes me
hollows me as a vessel
to pour His love through.

His fingerprints remain,
never erased with each carving.
proof that He is my Father,
and I am His daughter.

as long as I am being molded,
I know I am still being held.
the shaping,
the molding,
are proof His hands
are still upon me.

when His hands remain on me,
I am safe,
I am enough,
I am equipped.

I am fearfully,
wonderfully made,
formed by the Potter
for every purpose He designed me to be.

//

this space feels uncomfortable,
this unknown feeling is defeating.
it seems the only constant
in my life, are these tears.
while I know You are the constant
and the source of my peace -
my eyes are tired of looking up,
only to be blinded by the sun,
instead of warmed by You.
I know You are there,
You said so -
but You couldn't feel any further
away from me.

when I scream out to You, Lord,
why can't I hear You answer me?
the joy is gone, the pain is present,
I should be locked in on You -
but I'm rooted in this pain.
I'm scared of what's to come,
grieving what is already done,
stuck in a wave of tears
that makes home in my eyes.
my prayers and praises,
are they making their way to Heaven?
because this life
at times,
feels like I'm speaking into voids.
I want to feel Your presence, Lord,
I want to be heard -
can You hear me?

//

surrender feels strange -
when I've carried my own
strength for so long.
Lord, my striving can't save me,
only You can.
here I am
with my mustard seed,
although small,
in Your strong and mighty hands,
although quiet,
my whisper into Your ears,
I believe You can take my life,
and make it new.

from the very beginning,
You have only ever wanted this -
   - my happiness
   - my wholeness
   - my joy
breathe into me, Lord,
Your peace into my lungs.
every inhale and exhale,
the kind that only Heaven carries.
take my fears, Lord,
perform what only Your hands can do.
only You know,
the plans You have for me
   I surrender.
every thought,
breath,
word,
may they become nothing but You.
turn my fear into peace,
turn my voice into prayer.

//

my waiting is not punishment,
it carries no harsh sting
from God.
there is no cruel silence
no moment where our arms
aren't locked together.
though my ears may echo
with defeat
your word rings true -
this silence is holy,
Your pause is preparation.
my heart - not yet ready
to receive the wonders
of Your promises.
Lord, Your quiet
does not mean distance,
for You have never been closer.
your breath slips between my fingers,
closer than my very own breath
leaving my lungs and parted lips.
not only do You hold my dreams,
You hold me.

stacking my character,
building blocks of my future.
from sand to temple,
dust to trust -
one day I will walk
fully equipped.
these delays are not denials,
but threads of Your tapestry,
so divine -
my broken heart,
only heard *no*
You whispered, *not yet*
just like being formed
in the womb of my mother -
I grew with time.
teach me to rest in Your arms,
when I try to take the pen
from Your hands
and write my own story.
tend to me, my Gardener,
until I bloom in Your time.

//

though my heart aches with desire,
to become a mom someday,
I turn my eyes to You -
the Keeper of my tomorrow.
though I long to hold a piece of me,
with a desire bigger than my soul,
your timing is bigger -
the Author of my story.
I will worship Your promise
in my waiting.
teach me servanship, Lord,
teach me to serve You
while I wait.
the plans You have for me,
do not unravel overtime,
they unfold, perfectly.

every second You hold me,
is every second You hold my dreams.
why use the breath of my lungs for complaining,
when I could use my voice for prayer?
though I long to hear the word mama,
ring beautifully from a tiny voice,
I know You are not withholding,
but preparing.
just like You knit me
in the womb of my mother,
Your faithfulness is blooming inside of me.
Your presence is my promise,
I know You are knitting my story too.

//

Holy Water Page

"For I know the plans I have for you, declares the Lord, plans to prosper you and not to harm you, plans to give you hope and a future." — Jeremiah 29:11

Dream Mapping with God

This exercise isn't about forcing our desires, or pushing our own agenda into the hands of God, but more so opening our hearts to see how our desires align with His will. There is nothing wrong with having big dreams and aspirations, we just want to make sure that our eyes and hearts are open to what kind of future God wants us to have.

Prayer

Lord, every dream that I have belongs first to You. I know that through You, I will have the wisdom to know which of my desires are part of Your plan and which ones I need to release. While I understand that it is not easy to let go of my own fleshly wants and desires, help me to do so with ease, knowing You have a greater plan for me than I could ever imagine. Along the way, help me to trust Your timing, Your guidance, and Your love as I step into the future that You are writing for me. Amen

Journaling

1. What dream has the biggest tug on your heart right now? Write it down and ask God to speak into it.

    a. Note: God may speak to you in different ways. Keep your eyes on Him and the answers will be revealed.

2. Do any of your dreams feel like they were planted by God?

    a. Note: Your dreams won't just be for you solely, but on a broader level. How will your dreams help you to serve others? Can you use this gift so that it brings praise to God?

3. Are there any doubts that arise for you? Do you feel like these dreams are too far out of reach? Tell them to God.

4. Write your own prayer using this prompt to begin: "Lord, if this dream is in alignment with Your will....."

Sacred Action

→ In the first circle, write down your dreams, desires, and goals. This circle will be used to pray over daily.
→ Leave circle two blank. This circle will be used to fill in the dreams that God will reveal in His timing. There may be things He plants into your heart after prayer.

→ Pray over circle one: *"Lord, if these dreams are in alignment with Your plans for me, reveal them to me."* You may use any word choices that feel comfortable for you for this prayer!
→ Invite God into circle two: *"Lord, surprise me with Your vision for my life. I am open to what I can't yet see and trust that You are taking care of my future."*

✝ I like dream mapping because it acknowledges our human nature to have dreams and desires, but, most importantly, we also get to make space for God's unexpected plans. Your dreams aren't being dismissed but highlighted or transformed into something better.

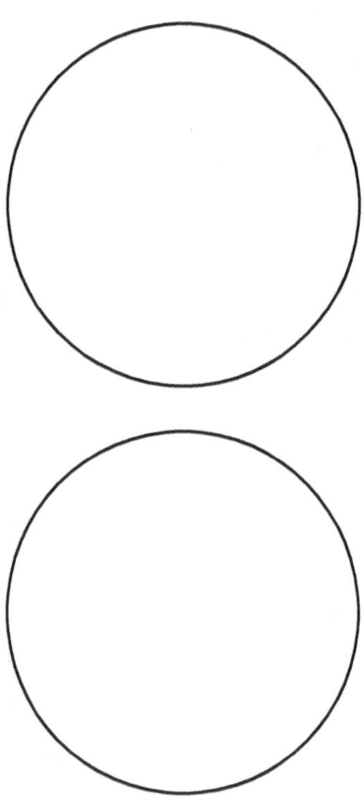

Stillness in the Psalms

Jesus,
a shoreline of safety -
the net that catches our falls -
flowing like a gentle stream.
Jesus,
a soft place to land -
the light on our shadows -
He who knows us by name.
Jesus,
our redeemer -
our healer -
our gardener.

Jesus,
He frees us -
He saves us-
He tends to us.
Jesus,
what a beautiful name it is!

//

Jesus,
to be in Your presence,
would undo my whole being.

I know I would
fold at my knees -
using the hem of Your garment
to dry the tears falling
from my face.

I would press myself against You,
longing to melt into the light
that You radiate.
just wanting to become one
with the love You have always given -
a love that never let me go.

I don't believe I would be brave enough,
oh, Lord -
to lift my eyes towards You.
I'd stare at Your feet,
the very feet that walked miles
by my side.
never stopping,
never leaving.

I'd trace them with my trembling hands,
retracing every step You took with me.
every step that carried me through desserts,
rollings waves,
and long valleys.

I'd wrap every inch of my being
around Your waist.
waiting for eternity to collapse
into this one embrace.

my heart would rumble like thunder
listening to the beat of Yours.
there is no language,
no rehearsal, no
experience on Earth,
that could prepare my ears
for the sound of Your voice.

oh the breath
I will exhale,
when I lean into You -
at last,
finally home.

//

My unfiltered letter to Jesus -

About my father.

I know You created me, like a flower to bloom, but my father left me unwatered. I felt no more a flower than a weed, that got stuck between the cracks of concrete, unworthy of being planted in gardens. I waited for him to show up - I prayed that he would come. I counted stars to pass the time, instead of sheep to fall asleep - hoping that the time would pass and he'd be there at the doorstep. As a little girl, I could not grasp the idea of his absence, or better yet, why he was okay with staying away. How could a parent bring life into this world and not want to see the life they helped create? Jesus, I know You have the answers, why can't You tell me so? I'm well into my thirties now and the distance he's created no longer haunts my dreams like when I was 10, but I have the rest of my life to sit and ponder what kept him away. What a life it has been. Learning the meaning of betrayal before even learning words. I became more fluent in waiting than I did my primary language. Numbers came easily because I got good at counting the hours he had been gone. No child should ever wonder if they are worthy of love - but I did. I think my heart aches for that little girl who never quite gave up waiting. That little girl still waits sometimes because she knows what it feels like when you finally lose hope. It's exhausting to keep holding on but how do I tell that sweet girl it's time to let go? His instability trained me to desire holding things together, or in other words, I became a perfectionist. I spent years trying to prove that I was enough, and when someone left, I failed my mission. Learning to dissociate was the coolest magic trick I had ever performed. Who wouldn't want to leave their body when the emotional weight got to be too heavy? Jesus, just tell me why. That's all I need to know; I won't ask anymore questions. Or maybe you can tell me why. Why that precious flower of a little girl never knew what number to call when she wanted her dad and how she never actually knew where he lived - here in the same town as her. Why did she randomly run into him in public and instantly swell with forgiveness instead of hatred? Why does a man who never showed up get so much of my grace? I know these things I may never know, so I bring my prayer to You. I know You saw the times I waited at the doorstep so I bring You this wound. Please water what he left to dry. I no longer want to be that little girl with empty arms and a time clock spent waiting. Jesus, please gather the wind that stole my petals, and return them back to me, make me whole again. With Your love, nothing withers, help me believe that truth. My mother did her best, oh Lord, You blessed me with a wonderful mom, and for that I thank You. She gathered all the love she had, and gave it to us. Thank You for the gift of her but I also pray for my mother, she had to do it alone and I know it wasn't always easy. Please fill her heart with joy, so the fear, pain, and struggle no longer cling to her soul. Amen

a dangerous prayer,
the kind where God is ready to move,
but are we ready for His movement?
dangerous prayers come wrapped in discomfort,
telling God, I know I need formed
but the molding I am not ready for.
I must fully surrender,
and that feels like being unbuckled
on a roller coaster backwards.
    terrifying!
but the dangerous prayers change us,
move us,
free us,
by revealing our hidden sins
and selfish motives,
making way to eternal life.

//

I know God exists -
but if I didn't,
my grandparents would be proof
that He does.

//

lately, I've been carrying a sadness
I cannot name.

my marriage is abundant,
my family is healthy,
the roof above me in tact,
yet still—
my spirit aches.

why does sorrow slip in
when blessings surround me?
why does the world lose its color?
even the buds on my tongue,
have lost their taste for life.

everything feels muted,
I hardly know who I am anymore.
my personality wears different masks
with every person I meet.
big crowds are either loud to the ears,
or too quiet for the soul, rattling the frailest of bones.
sometimes being among people
feels more dangerous
than solitude itself.
but if the people don't consume me,
my thoughts certainly will.

I am a sensitive soul,
my tears flow freely like rivers.
but they never fall gently
like streams over smooth stones.
these tears of mine come running
as if the river can't meet the ocean quick enough.
I want this unexplainable sadness
to cease.
and long for unexplainable happiness
to take its place—
the kind that
even when the roof caves in,
the kind that
even when the kitchen is bare,
my happiness is still alive.
the kind of joy not bound
to circumstances,
but tethered only to His light.

//

✝ Lord, when waves of unexplainable sadness hit my soul like sea storms, please fill my space with Your healing waters. Guide me to waters that are still & calm. Protect me from my thoughts that do not reflect the love You have for me. Block every fear, doubt, and worry that my soul carries. I know You are with me everywhere I go. Lead my steps to walk towards you, not only when I'm sad but when I'm happy too. Amen

"The Lord is close to the brokenhearted and saves those who are crushed in spirit." — Psalm 34:18

the act of growing old with you sounds romantic - timeless,
a true love story for all ages,
but I would be lying if I said it didn't come with a little fear.
when I'm 80, I'll dream of the night we slept under the stars
in the bed of your chevy pickup,
candles adorned the space, a mosquito net built just for me, a
projector and our favorite show.
on the days when old age begins to catch up,
I'll look at your face and remember the youth it carried,
and I will think about the pets we had that have long since
passed & remember the fun they brought to our 30's.
but darling, I'm a little scared,
when I think about who will go first.
I love you too much to leave you here behind,
grieving me,
but my heart isn't strong enough to be here without you...
so maybe we will go together.
maybe your last breath on Earth will be mine too.

//

✝ Lord, thank You for the gift of my spouse. Help me to cherish every day that we have together and to never take their love for granted. Guide our love to grow stronger through You as each day passes. Help us to hold onto each other with gratitude, as we hold onto You with trust. Until it is our time, please help us savor every day that is granted and when our last breath is taken on Earth, may it be filled with peace, knowing our next one will be with You. Help us to understand that the love we have is a glimpse of eternal life that we will get to enjoy together. Amen

"A cord of three strands is not easily broken." - Ecclesiastes 4:12

God knows what He is doing -
He knows that once I find comfort,
I cling to it like glue.
safety nets are my thing,
steady ground is my security.
& I will not move—
unless the moving truck is packed,
and even then,
my foot is heavy on the brakes.

God needs me to move,
because He just knows what stillness can steal.
so He calls me to move.
He calls me to change.

and sometimes moving means breaking—
it sometimes comes with losing.
it comes with pain that scrapes the soul raw,
and even means leaving some people behind.
but even in the midst of pain,
it comes with Him.
kneeling at our side,
and collecting the shards of our brokenness -
with his strong and mighty hands.
only He can make a broken heart new again.

hidden in every push,
His mercy waited in disguise.

each time He pried me from comfort,
something beautiful bloomed
on the other side.
not because He wanted me to suffer-
but because He wanted me to grow,
to become the daughter
He always knew I could be.

//

✝ Lord, help me to remember that I do not need to build my own safety nets for You are the only net I will ever need. When You call me to move, please help me do so with ease, knowing I am fully equipped because of Your grace. Guide me to trust in Your word, knowing You will never lead me astray. Help me to release the grip on anything that is not You and hold steady what is eternal. Lord, I trust that when things break, I am in good hands, for You are our builder. Help me let go of the old, for You already have crafted the new. Thank You for loving my heart back to life. Amen

"For I know the plans I have for you, declares the Lord, plans to prosper you and not to harm you, plans to give you hope and a future." - Jeremiah 29:11

dear friends,
take your time with these words.

this is not just another poem,
this is a call.
a call from Jesus,
a door He is holding open for you.

life is too short
to play safe on the sidelines.
Pray. Forgive. Repent. Serve.
The devil is busy,
but our Lord is busier.

The enemy will do everything
to distract your forgiving heart.
The walk with Jesus is beautiful—
but it is not without battle.

Keep your eyes on Jesus,
He will shield you from every wall,
every trap,
every cliff edge
That the enemy has built.

Let go of the world's grip;
it is only dust and smoke.
Tighten your grip,
that's all you need friends.
The fabric of your life
is already woven into His garment.
no enemy can unravel
what His love has already stitched.
Fix your eyes on Jesus, the time is here.

It only takes one step
in His direction.
One breath.
One yes
One I believe

Your yes to Jesus
is a doorway to forever—
but you must walk through,
Build your relationship with Him.
pray that your days
are filled with nothing but Him.
It's okay if this is your first time.
He has already run to meet you
long before you could turn the page.

The riches of this world
cannot compare
to the love He has for you.
The time is now—
make your heart right.
Forgive.

Ask the Lord for recalibration;
we cannot do this
by our own strength.
Pray for spiritual eyesight
to see beyond the physical world.

Hope glows on the horizon
for those who return to Him.
The invitation is still open.
His hand is reaching for you—
will you take it?

✝ Lord, today I say I do to You! Forgive me of my sins and help me make straight my path, my ways, and my heart. I come to You with a heart that is begging for forgiveness. I am sorry for my sins and I pray that You make my heart, my actions, and my mind, pure and filled with nothing but You. I want to walk this path with You. Please be with me every step of this journey so that I may be alert and ready for Your return, with a joyful heart.. Amen

"For I do not understand my own actions. For I do not do what I want, but I do the very thing I hate." - Romans 7:15

Even the apostle, Paul, struggled with His own sinfulness. Romans 7:15, one of my favorite verses, helps me to understand my story and how I carry my own sin.

Can you relate to Paul? I know I can. Why is it so easy for me to sin sometimes? Why is it hard to do the very thing I want to do but so easy for me to do the things I hate? I, like Paul, want to follow God's law, draw near to Jesus, and never sin again but my physical nature does the opposite. Our flesh still pulls us in a direction far from Jesus but He's still near to us - for our dependance on Him will help us weed out our sin.

I love this scripture because of the rawness behind it. Every believer struggles between stumbling into sin and loving God. Feeling shame for loving God but still choosing to sin but true victory over sin rests not in ourselves but in Christ. When we remember that it is not us who can defeat it but the power of the Holy Spirit, the flesh becomes less porous and open to sin.

Thanks be to God, we see proof of our defeat over sin in Romans 6:14: *"For sin shall no longer be your master, because you are not under the law, but under grace."* We as believers are no longer slaves to sin because of the transformative power of grace. How beautiful is that! This encourages us to live a life of holiness as we are called to live by the Spirit. His Grace sanctifies us! We are free from the bondage of sin as we rely on His grace daily for strength and guidance in overcoming sin.

    surrender the weight
too heavy to carry,
let it slide from your shoulders and into His hands.
can you see how time has tired you?
how your bones ache
from burdens not yours to keep?

forgive,

so the war inside your heart may cease.
forgiveness is the breath
that clears the smoke from our lungs,
it quiets the fire
that once burned your soul.

and love—
love again,
for love is what makes the world spin.
the orbit itself
is carried by His mercy.
the very gravity that holds us
is nothing but love
love is not just a word, it is who He is.

//

surrender - make room for Jesus to dance in your heart.

forgive - make room for Jesus to fill your lungs with peace.

love - make room for Jesus to grow lilies within your soul.

//

we are only as rich, as our trust in the Lord.

the gold of this world
cannot compare
to the gold in His heart.

if our hearts beat for Him,
the Earth's heartbeat
learns how to heal.

imagine—
a world rich in love,
not possessions.
a wealth beyond coins,
beyond crowns,
beyond all earthly treasures.

for a heart that beats for God
is a heart that cannot be bought,
a heart that cannot be sold.

the way Jesus loves us
is beyond every jewel,
His love for us, an inheritance eternal,
a treasure without end.
we are spiritually rich,
because He is alive in me and You.

//

have You not heard my prayers, Lord?
do You not see my longing—
how I am drawn to motherhood
like bees to pollen?

the positive tests surrounding me,
are they only tests?
am I failing in faith?
a baby feels so far away -

others hold bold blue lines,
my vision blurs
beneath their announcements.
did You not form me,
to bear a child?

this is at the top of every list at Christmas,
copy and paste every year that passes.

I see the lights on the tree
and think of the star
that led the Magi to You—
the miracle.
is it wrong to ask for my own miracle too?
have You turned off the porch light?
are You still there?

I dream of little toes

leaving prints on my heart,
hands that will reach for mine,
a laugh I can already hear
but not yet hold.
to hear "Mama" for the first time—
oh Lord, I ache for it.

//

forgive me the times I doubted You-
for Your wisdom surpasses my lack.
Your timing surpasses my impatience.
prepare me for motherhood,
heal me so my child
finds a home of love inside me.

help me be still while You work,
if the waves obey Your voice, so can I.

point me back to You,
the only North I need,
my true compass.
teach me to praise You while I wait.
remind me, delay is not denial.
make my waiting
a sanctuary.
breathe peace into my lungs
so I can exhale trust
instead of fear.

//

but Jesus, who am I to write this book?
the woman I am calling you to be -
He replied.
as fallen people,
living in a fallen world,
we will never feel adequate enough,
our shame will wrap itself around
and weigh us down like damp linens.
here is the catch,
if we could land on the moon,
and shoot for the stars on our own,
Jesus wouldn't exist.
our identity isn't in this world,
but in He, who created this Earth.

//

Holy Water page:

I know this season of waiting feels hard, especially when all we hear is silence. Whether you are waiting on a child, a transplant, for healing, change, a partner... He's still here. The porch light is still on. Waiting is the most important time we are offered. It is within the waiting, we build strength, a change of heart, a new perspective, and transformation. The soil is where the true growth takes place. Surrender your calendar to Him!

Exercise

For this exercise, you are going to do what I call a labyrinth prayer. It's simple and easy to do wherever you are whenever you need. Extra labyrinths will be in the back of the book for when you need them and available for download. With a pen or pencil, you will trace the path until you get to the center, repeating *Lord, You are enough, Lord, I trust in Your timing,* or *Lord, You are the way, the truth, and the life.* You can use any word choices that feel comfortable for you. When you make it to the center, spend some time with Him, thanking Him for the journey, as the labyrinth is a metaphor for the journey you are taking with Him by your side every step. Then when you are ready, you will trace your way back to the beginning of the labyrinth. This time, thanking Him for the journey, praying for the needs of the people in your life, and expressing your love for this life.

To start, take a deep breath, let go of any distractions like phone and TV, and surrender this moment to Him.

You may play soft music in the background before you start to help calm your mind. Take your time, there is no rush to get to the center!

Start here!

Anastasia Lindsey

Stillness
in the Psalms

Stillness in the Psalms

Stillness in the Psalms

   speaking of light,
it finally came on for me.
I am not part of the crowd,
I am part of His light
that help leads the way.
all this time,
I have placed my focus on being
the one that doesn't quite fit in.
it was the curse that kept me shackled
to the weight of my own misunderstanding.
because I am so deep, I've always been left behind
in what felt like dark and cold waters.
what I missed was that I am the feelings
that people haven't quite found the words to yet.
to me, the world has always been too loud,
too distracted.
every fine detail gets missed between the cracks
of broken hearts and concrete slabs.
my nervous system is like an instrument
so finely tuned into every note,
every detail.

not every ear is primed for such beauty.
solitude has always replenished me,
yes, that I know -
but it didn't come without feelings of emptiness.
where I saw empty, was really healing space,
a sacred invitation for stillness
in a world that is constantly on the go.
it is in those spaces where the quiet voice
of my soul can truly speak the loudest.
my sensitive nature may have kept me apart
but it always drew me in to those who needed
authentic eyes, and a soft space to land on.
    He knew what He was doing, when He created me

//

my soul has been shattered
into pieces, time and time again.
some pieces return, others find new homes.
some come back changed—
what I once knew to be true
shifts quietly into another belief.

things that once mattered
fade like ink in rain.
when I think one ache has ended,
another knocks gently at the door.

the day my grandmother left this world,
I was fourteen and unfinished.
pieces of me left that day too—
before I had the chance
to fully know who I was becoming.
eighteen years later,
I still look in the mirror
and see the hollows where her laughter used to live.

relationships, friendships—
those too have come and gone.
people with *forever* written on their hearts
turned out to be passing seasons.
I've watched their footprints wash away
before I could memorize the sound of their joy.

at thirty-one, I lost my grandpa.
a different kind of grief found me then—
older, quieter, but heavy enough
to take not just pieces, but handfuls.
leaving that old job years ago
felt the same,
grief disguised as freedom,
comfort mistaken for calling.
lightning struck the ground of my certainty,
and still I stayed to watch it burn.

but through it all, I have come to understand
that grief is not the end of the story—
it's the garden where Jesus plants new things,
He is the King of Restoration.
the One who gathers our fragments
and names them whole.
the One who fills our hollow spaces
with living water.
the One who takes our nothing
and calls it something sacred.

//

in poetry, we say, *loneliness is eating at my bones,*
God says, *do not fear, I am with you. Isaiah 41:10*
in poetry, we say, *I feel insecure,*
God says, *you are fearfully and wonderfully made. Psalm 139:14*
in poetry, *we say, fear has taken my light,*
God says, *my rod and my staff will comfort you. Psalm 23:4*
in poetry, we say, *my finances have left me dry,*
God says, *I will supply your every need. Philippians 4:19*
in poetry, we say, *I wear my shame loudly,*
God says, *you are now free from condemnation. Romans 8:1-17*
in poetry, we say, *my mind is occupied with worry and anxiety,*
God says, *I have clothed the grass, therefore I shall clothe you too.*
Matthew 6:25-34

//

I was never good at math,
good thing!
the only equation I will ever need
is enough to save my soul.
Jesus,
the Way + The Truth = The Life.
He is The Sum, The Total,
& The Answer that solves every unknown.

//

He took my blank slate, my human soul,
and begin to fill the space with color.
if you were to see me, in this very moment,
my canvas would appear messy,
still dripping with yesterday's paint
and no clear vision of what I am becoming.
each day, He gathers His thoughts at the easel,
picking up His brushes with mercy in His hands,
every stroke of the bristles
carries a part of my story.
I am both the canvas, and the creation -
who I become, is all in His hands.

He took the Earth's sun,
and brought light to my blank spaces.
took the Earth's sacred ground,
and molded the brown of my eyes.
the same hands that formed the elements,
were used to form me.
although my canvas
is still a work in progress -
there is sanctification in every stroke.
what looks unfinished to me,
is already complete to Him.
in His artistry,
I am being made holy.

//

Holy Water Page!

If you're anything like me, you have spent most of your life trying to solve God - or better yet, you tried to solve your life's problems yourself, and maybe both. You may have tried to earn your peace on Earth by coming up with your own formulas. It's okay, I have done it too. I am here to assure you that there is only one equation that leads us to true peace.

The Holy Equation *

    The Way + The Truth = The Life.
    He is The Sum of every variable and character.

Reflection:

In the first two blanks below, write things you have tried to add together, hoping that they would bring you something (the 3rd blank).

My example: Good deeds + Approval = Success & Peace

_________________ + _________________ = _________________

Now, I want you to cross out the equation gently, and beneath it write:

The Way + The Truth = The Life.

Whisper it like a prayer, sing it like a song, believe it like the truth. Let your soul remember that because He is The Way, you will always have the truth. Because He is The Truth, you will always have life. Because He is The Life, you will always know the way.

Prayer:

Say to yourself quietly or out loud: "I surrender every formula that I have ever created that excluded You, Lord. Please forgive me relying on my own strength and not that of Yours. You are The Answer to every unknown and The Bringer of peace. I have tried to formulate my worth, by adding things that never satisfied me. Thank you for being The Equation that equals everything I am, and everything I am made to be. Help me, Lord, to rest in Your Totality. Amen.

I was sleepwalking for too long,
dismissing my sin as if grace were a blanket
that I used to hide what I refused to uncover.
saying to myself, *I'm forgiven,* so it's okay
comparing my wrongs to another's,
believing that their weeds were more overgrown than mine.
most of my life, repentance felt like routine,
something I did out of obligation,
not out of ache.

now, every sin sits heavy on my heart,
so I lay them at His feet begging for forgiveness,
not because I deserve a cleansed heart,
but because He deserves my heart's surrender.
press me, Lord,
make new wine out of me.
help me weed out sin,
for I do not want to take your death for granted,
but every time I chose sin,
that's exactly what I am doing.
I dig deep,
down to the root of my rebellion,
cure the rot beneath the surface, Lord,
do not let it choke my garden of faith.
through Your Word, I am watered,
through Your mercy, I am blooming.
teach me to sow righteousness,
to bear fruit worthy of Your sunlight.

//

I do not fear the dark,
for God's light once walked this Earth.
Jesus pierced the darkness
of a world once decaying,
and left behind His glow,
a lantern in the chest of believers.

//

Inspired by John 1:5

Jesus,
the only contract I will ever need.
He signs His name in mercy,
not by my perfection,
but by His grace.
Jesus,
the only contract I will ever need,
He stamps His name with authority,
not with conditions,
but with love.

//

Jesus,

He met my younger self in a dream
and I stood there with a heart half-formed,
already shaped by fear.
He took my trembling hand and said
you don't have to be brave here.
He could call each tear by name,
before I could place them in His palms.
the chaos of my environment roared around us
as He slipped a pair of headphones over my ears.
together we sat in silence,
listening to a sound only Heaven could make.
before I spoke,
His eyes met mine with gentle grace,
I know. It wasn't your fault.
tears puddled my eyes
like a rainy April day.
how did He know?
I offered Him picked daisies,
broken little petals of gratitude.
you don't need to perform to receive my love.

that was the sweetest way anyone
had ever said thank you before.
what about my sensitivity?
I had the courage to ask.
your big feelings aren't a burden,
they are rivers that help others bloom.
just you wait and see.
people will feel safe in your presence,
that is how you will change the world.
and I believed Him.
every word.
before my eyes could open,
He placed my hand over my heart,
repeat after me.
I am loved by Jesus
He is never far from my heart.
and when I awoke,
the warmth of His love was still there.
reminding me, as an adult,
not once had I ever been alone.

//

we do not speak enough
about the weight of the cross.
not just the wood,
but every feeling of guilt that sin brought
was placed on the cross that day.
His flesh torn,
where perfection once rested.
Heaven's heart broken,
by Earth's hatred and rejection.
the cross did not simply lie gently on His back,
it pierced open wounds,
the splinters found a new home.
just to take a breath,
to bring air into His lungs
presented a new torture unknown to man.
His perfection wore pain,
His Holiness endured the sting of human confusion.
mocked by the ones He came to save,
pain that could not be measured justly,
the kind that no heart can fully carry.
dear reader,
He knows the sting of being unseen,
the ache of being abandoned,
how it feels when betrayal bleeds from the body.
when your breathing feels like breaking,
when grief wraps around your ribs,
He's closest to your sorrow, you are not alone.
the man who carried the weight of world's sin,
can carry your pain away.

//

JESUS IS
FLUENT IN
TEARS

scripture stitches a broken heart
with threads of His living light.
it takes our straight lines,
the paths we take from our own understanding,
and bends them back to Him.

the Bible meets us in our chaos,
reminding us we are His creation.
His words spill off the page,
and floods broken homes,
broken hearts,
and crashes into doors once closed.
every psalm is a map,
every parable a letter,
that leads us back into the hands that created us.
His words are proof that love existed
long before my eyes had sight.

//

I want my poetry to be soaked with Jesus,
drenched with His love,
and overflowing with His forgiveness.

//

I have big dreams on my heart,
a God-calling so loud,
its tunes rattle my ribs.
a tune so loud,
it can only come from His lips.
my human hands tremble beneath it,
as I try to keep from spilling His vision.
the dream that lingers in my mind,
is His reflection living inside,
therefore my hands will never fumble,
the dreams that fit in His palms.
Proverbs 28:19,
where there is no vision, the people perish
His breath is the very force that drives me forward.

//

if something breaks my Lord's heart,
I want it to break mine too.
not to shatter me into pieces,
but to reconstruct my heart
to be more like His.

//

I will give you a new heart and put a new spirit in you; I will remove from you your heart of stone and give you a heart of flesh. - Ezekiel 36:26

your value is not measured by perfection,
His perfect hands formed you.
your worth is not earned by performance,
His love says you already inherited it.
your progress is not an uncomplete project,
His promise was fulfilled before your first breath

//

Holy water page:

This exercise is called The Empty Chair Encounter. You can either visualize yourself and Jesus sitting in these chairs on the next page, or grab a physical chair for you and the other for Jesus, and imagine Him there. This is an opportunity to sit with Jesus, even though His presence is invisible, it can be felt! It's easy to feel like the distance between your heart and Heaven is far, this visualization can help bridge the gap. When you pull a chair for Jesus, you are actively saying: *You are welcome here, Lord. I believe You are with me.*

What do you want to talk to Him about? What is heavy on your heart? This can be used for anything. You can even sit in silence while you feel His love.

If you would like, you can hold a notebook and pen, have The Bible at your side, or whatever will help you hear Him. Allow yourself to be surprised at what will come through as you lean into Him and His presence

Reflection questions:

> → What did I feel or sense in His presence?
> → Did He show me any truths or share any insight?
> → How does my heart feel, after having spent some time with Him?

The Empty Chair Encounter

Anastasia Lindsey

Stillness *in the Psalms*

When to trust God:

in the waiting
in the quiet
during the storms
when the answer is no
when the answer is yes
when He turns and says, not yet
in the middle of the night
in the midst of grief
during your trials
when the world stops spinning
when the mind overwhelms you
when you cannot feel Him
in the middle of heartbreak
in time of suffering
during seasons of slowness and slumber

In their hearts humans plan their course, but the Lord establishes their steps. - Proverbs 16:9

//

when I chose to follow Jesus,
He began to strip me of distractions.
what I saw as isolation,
He called freedom.
the things I used to love,
the comforts that I longed for,
He plucked one by one.
what I saw as silence,
He called freedom
the more He stripped away,
the more He was revealed.
what I once relied on for comfort,
was replaced with reliance on Christ.
He pried my fingers from false security,
from everything that was not Him.
He became my provider,
my strength,
my source,
the pulse of my heart.
everything I lost,
was a clearing for His light to reach me.
when He called me close,
I did not push away.
the quiet that followed
revealed a gentle truth.
what I thought was isolation,
was only an invitation -
I wasn't losing my life,
I was just finding it in Him.

//

I know what it feels like to want His healing,
what it feels like to be sick, diagnosed,
what suffering feels like in the body,
just longing for His hands to cover your wounds.
the salt of your tears sting the skin,
the old ones, not yet dry.
I too dream of an anointing,
just a drop of His living water,
to cover what aches inside.
if your pain is like mine,
it moves throughout the body
and wraps around the bones.
the bitterness of being human
feels like a cross too heavy to carry.
I long to feel His fingerprints pressed
against my wounds,
to be healed by His word alone.

stand with me,
lets believe together,
that one day He will come
and His hands will heal
what medicine could not.
our hearts may ache,
but what good are they
if we do not believe in Him?
I know the pain is real,
and the diagnosis is heavy,
but a crushed spirit will dry the bones
much quicker than any illness.
rejoice, beloved,
we know a Savior.
we know a Healer.
rest in that today.

//

I imagine the shoreline of Heaven,
where things of the Earth fall away,
and tears are dried
before our feet touch the sand.
the breeze whispers of forgiveness,
and the waves are gentle,
they sound like home.
I imagine the water in Heaven,
has replaced the salt with sugar
and here, eternity is sweet,
the air is pure.
gold spills into the lungs
when filled with God's breath.
here, the sky surrounds the shore,
folding into endless clouds of love.
loved ones greet us with joy,
their footprints pressed in the sand
of His eternal beach.

//

we are like rivers,
winding along the cracks of Earth,
carving our pain into stones
crashing into sorrow,
making our way to the Father at sea,
where the sinner meets the Forgiver.
some of us have flowed in the same river
for many years.
circling what seemed to be endless miles
of dirty water that clogged our pores.
for so long we forgot what it felt like
to be clear, because of Him.
there He waits,
where our waters will soon meet,
arms open,
tides willing and wide.
the currents of His mercy
washing away everything unclean.
not too cast shame on our uncleanliness,
but to remind us, we can always flow home.

//

Holy Water Page

One of my favorite things to do are faith based affirmations. There isn't a right or wrong way to say them, just be comfortable! I like to play soft music while I recite mine, but you can do what feels best for you. Saying them in bed before you start your day is a great way! I have included scriptures that anchor the Word to your heart.

→ I let the current wash away what no longer serves the Lord's purpose for my life.
Scripture says: *"He leads me beside still waters; He restores my soul."* - Psalm 23:2-3

→ I am made whole through Him.
Scripture says: *"By His wounds we are healed."* - Isaiah 53:5

→ I flow with the Lord, wherever I go.
Scripture says: *"In all your ways acknowledge Him, and He will make straight your paths."*- Proverbs 3:6

→ The Lord is my home, I am safe here.
Scripture says: *"Lord, you have been our dwelling place throughout all generations."* - Psalm 90:1

→ I meet the Lord at sea, He washes me clean.
Scripture says: *"Wash me, and I shall be whiter than snow."* - Psalm 51:7

→ My identity resides in the heart of Jesus.
Scripture says: *"For you died, and your life is now hidden with Christ in God." -* Colossians 3:3

→ I can do all things through Christ who strengthens me.
Scripture says: *"I can do all things through Christ who strengthens me." -* Philippians 4:13

→ God hears my requests and answers my prayers.
Scripture says: *"Before they call I will answer, while they are still speaking I will hear." -* Isaiah 65:24

→ He keeps His promises and does what He says.
Scripture says: *"Not one of all the Lord's good promises to Israel failed; every one was fulfilled." -* Joshua 21:45

→ For when I fix my eyes on the Lord, my feet never stumble.
Scripture says: *"When you walk, your steps will not be hindered; and when you run, you will not stumble." -* Psalm 121:3

→ The weapons formed against me will never prosper.
Scripture says: *"No weapon formed against you shall prosper." -* Isaiah 54:17

→ I am God's masterpiece!
Scripture says: *"For we are His workmanship, created in Christ Jesus for good works." -* Ephesians 2:10

→ He establishes my steps and leads me to the path of righteousness.

Scripture says: *"The steps of a good man are ordered by the Lord, and He delights in his way."* - Psalm 37:23

Stillness
in the Psalms

Beloved reader,

may the Lord bless you on this journey—
in the stillness and in the storm.
may you remember that you are never walking alone;
your steps are guided by hands that have never lost their way.

when life feels heavy,
may you feel His nearness in the quiet corners of your day.
when joy overflows,
may you lift your eyes to the Giver of all good things
and say *thank You.*

may your prayers become rivers,
flowing endlessly into His sea of mercy.
may your faith deepen like roots
and your hope rise like dawn.

I pray that you fall in love with Him—
deeply, daily, without fear.
that your life becomes a psalm itself,
a living prayer that points others toward the Light.

and when the tide feels too strong,
when you forget the way home,
may you always find yourself
on the shoreline of His grace—
safe, seen, and forever loved.
In Jesus' name,

Amen

Here are some of my favorite verses. My poetry book would be nothing but verses if I put every verse that I loved. My hope is that as you read through these, you dive deeper into the Bible and find ones that then become your favorite too!

Psalm 147:3: "He heals the brokenhearted and binds up their wounds."

Jeremiah 17:14: "Heal me, Lord, and I will be healed; save me and I will be saved, for you are the one I praise."

Mark 5:34: "He said to her, 'Daughter, your faith has healed you. Go in peace and be freed from your suffering.'"

Psalm 6:2: Be gracious to me, O Lord, for I am languishing; heal me, O Lord, for my bones are troubled.

Matthew 6:34 "Therefore do not worry about tomorrow, for tomorrow will worry about itself. Each day has enough trouble of its own."

Romans 8:38-39 "And I am convinced that nothing can ever separate us from God's love. Neither death nor life, neither angels nor demons, neither our fears for today nor our worries about tomorrow — not even the powers of hell can separate us from God's love. No power in the sky above or in the Earth below—indeed, nothing in all creation will ever be able to separate us from the love of God that is revealed in Christ Jesus our Lord."

John 16:33 "In the world you will have tribulation. But take heart; I have overcome the world."

Philippians 4:6–7 (NIV) Do not be anxious about anything, but in every situation, by prayer and petition, with thanksgiving, present your requests to God. And the peace of God, which transcends all understanding, will guard your hearts and your minds in Christ Jesus.

Joshua 1:9 "Have I not commanded you? Be strong and courageous. Do not be frightened, and do not be dismayed, for the LORD your God is with you wherever you go."

Philippians 2:3–4 "Do nothing from selfish ambition or conceit, but in humility count others more significant than yourselves. Let each of you look not only to his own interests, but also to the interests of others."

Jeremiah 29:11 "For I know the plans I have for you," declares the LORD, "plans to prosper you and not to harm you, plans to give you hope and a future."

Psalms 119:11 "Your word I have hidden in my heart, That I might not sin against You!"

Isaiah 40:31 "But those who wait on the LORD Shall renew their strength; They shall mount up with wings like eagles, They shall run and not be weary, They shall walk and not faint."

Matthew 1:21 "And she will bring forth a Son, and you shall call His name Jesus, for He will save His people from their sins."

Matthew 16:24-26 "Then Jesus said to His disciples, "If anyone desires to come after Me, let him deny himself, and take up his cross, and follow Me. "For whoever desires to save his life will lose it, but whoever loses his life for My sake will find it. "For what profit is it to a man if he gains the whole world, and loses his own soul? Or what will a man give in exchange for his soul?"

Luke 11:28 "But He said, "More than that, blessed are those who hear the word of God and keep it!"

Romans 8:28 "And we know that all things work together for good to those who love God, to those who are called according to His purpose."

1st Corinthians 3:16 "Do you not know that you are the temple of God and that the Spirit of God dwells in you?"

Galatians 2:20 "I have been crucified with Christ; it is no longer I who live, but Christ lives in me; and the life which I now live in the flesh I live by faith in the Son of God, who loved me and gave Himself for me."

Jame 4:8 "Draw near to God, and he will draw near to you."

Testimony Page:

What has He done for you throughout reading this book and beyond? Use this page to record your living miracles!

Anastasia Lindsey

Stillness in the Psalms

Join me for Saltwater Sunday's:

Follow me on IG where one Sunday a month, I will go live for reflections, prayers, poems, and more that will help us continue the journey together!

Scan the QR code below. See you there!

www.ingramcontent.com/pod-product-compliance
Lightning Source LLC
Chambersburg PA
CBHW051435130726
47987CB00005B/2060